First published by
Brewin Books Ltd, 56 Alcester Road,
Studley, Warwickshire B80 7LG in 2013
www.brewinbooks.com

ISBN: 978-1-85858-518-5

A Cataloguing in Publication Record
for this title is available from the British Library.

Typeset in Proxima Nova
Printed in Great Britain

BREWIN BOOKS

How to Potty train

We saw a need for an easy to follow guide to help explain the foundations for good potty training.

"How to Potty Train" will help you through the stages of potty training in our 5 easy steps. We've combined fun sections for children with tips and guidance for parents, so that you can learn together while enjoying the journey.

The most common question we get asked is "When should I start to potty train?" We help you identify the signs of readiness, and work with you right through - up to tackling night time potty training and beyond.

Parents are often blamed for potty training happening later and lasting longer. In our opinion, this trend is a direct result of the introduction and increased use of disposable nappies since the 1960s. While they are convenient, the very reason they are a success makes them ineffective for potty training.

Disposables are just too absorbent and dry for children to learn what their bodies are telling them. As a result, nappies mask the signs of readiness, which often sees them being used past the optimal time to potty train.

This prolonged use of nappies has created a whole set of new issues in relation to potty training and in this book we try to re-establish good common sense practices - practices that you can use on a day to day basis to make potty training easier.

A good routine is at the heart of potty training and our 'read together' story sections will help you explain the process to your child in a fun and engaging way.

We have worked together on Dry Like Me since 2008, and have met hundreds of health visitors and continence experts from all over the world. More importantly, we have also spoken to many parents who are tackling potty training. We know that potty training is often regarded as the most stressful part of parenting, and that there are times when parents just do not know where to turn for help and information.

We hope we have helped resolve this, and that "How to Potty Train" will now be a treasured aid to this important milestone.

Jude & Di

READ TOGETHER

We have designed the book to be enjoyed with your child.

The 'read together' sections will help instill good potty training habits and expectations.

Repetition is key so the more you read together the better.

Good Luck!

We have included lots of tip boxes for parents!

Our easy 5 step process

Work through these 5 easy steps to build confidence and establish good potty training habits.

1

Preparing

Page 6

This is all about getting ready for potty training, how to establish a good routine and preparing your child for the journey ahead.

2

Signs of readiness

Page 28

We help you recognise the signs of readiness so you are confident that you are ready to go for it. Knowing the optimum time to potty train your child and getting this right can make potty training happen faster.

"The journey of a thousand miles begins with one step" Lao Tzu

3

Going for it!

Page 34

This important step is all about making the leap into own pants and managing expectations for you and your child.

4

Keeping going

Page 42

Once you have mastered success at home the next step is keeping dry when out and about, and when there are lots of distractions.

5

Night Time

Page 48

This is the final step of potty training, usually tackled when the child is dry in the day.

Just like in daytime potty training, it is important to establish a good routine and manage expectations at night time.

Step 1

Preparing

> **"Success is the sum of small efforts, repeated day in and day out."**
> Robert Collier

You can start preparing to potty train from around 18 months, when your child is ready to take some simple direction and instructions. Your child may be reaching key milestones such as learning to walk, and learning to communicate, and may be showing an interest in being independent.

At this first stage of potty training, a child is learning to understand when they have done a wee, and how they recognise the difference between wet and dry. You will need to help them with this, as nappies make it very hard for them to feel the difference.

Potty training is also a learned experience (like learning to brush your teeth). So the very first stage is to teach your child a good routine, and set in place the habits and expectations that will help you successfully potty train.

Key tips:
- Change your child in the bathroom as this is where grown-ups go.
- Change your child standing up, to make them an active part of the process.
  (This signals a step away from having their nappy changed for them on the floor like a baby).
- Tell your child when a nappy is wet and when it is dry to help them learn.
- Encourage them to help with their own clothing.
- Talk to them when you go to the toilet, and tell them that wee and poo go down the loo.
- Make your language around toileting consistent.
- Buy a potty to keep in the bathroom to practice sitting on. Use it in the morning and before bath time.
- Don't put them under pressure. Praise the practice and the effort.

Read Poppy and Pablo's big routine together with your child and put the routine in place straight away!

The goal and the signs you are ready to move to the next stage is that your child can recognise and tell you...

I've done a wee.

Poppy and Pablo's
Big Routine

Poppy and Pablo are going to show you all about potty training.

And do lots of fun grown up things.

Because then you can wear your grown up pants.

TIP: Help your child name some people they know who don't wear nappies, such as friends, relatives, or a favourite TV character...

When you wear a nappy you can wee and poo anywhere!

Grown ups use the bathroom when they go to the toilet.

Wee and Poo belong in the loo!

TIP: In future change your child's nappy in the bathroom, remind them wee and poo belongs in the loo! Going in a nappy is easy as someone else clears up the mess.

Did you know that your body speaks to you every day? If you listen hard it will tell you when it is time to go to the toilet.

It tells you when you are tired ...YAWWWN!

It tells you when you are hungry ...grrrr.

It secretly tells you when you need the toilet!

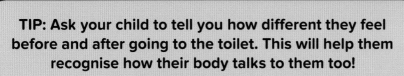

TIP: Ask your child to tell you how different they feel before and after going to the toilet. This will help them recognise how their body talks to them too!

Everybody goes to the toilet.
When you eat your body keeps all the good stuff
to make you healthy, and give you energy,
but it has to get rid of all the waste.

Everybody's wee and poo goes to the same place!

Even the Queen!?

TIP: If your child has a favourite person or character explain that they too have to go to the toilet and it is perfectly normal!

When you learn to use the toilet you might like to buy some special things to help you...

Grown up pants

A potty

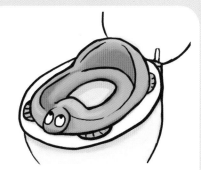

A special seat for the toilet

A step stool

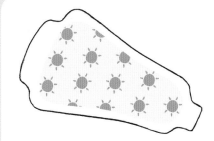

Dry Like Me potty training pads

Some nice toddler wipes, and handwash.

TIP: Have fun letting your child help choose their new potty training kit, it will motivate them...

When you start to potty train you can say
"bye bye" to your nappy.
You will now be a very grown up person.
You will still use a nappy at night though....

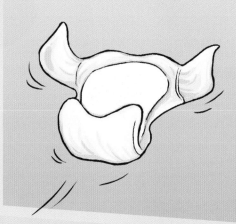

Goodbye
Nappy!!!

TIP: Be clear with your child
that from now on there are no
nappies in the day, you could
even make a fuss of throwing
them out!

You will have lots of accidents to begin with,
that's ok! Just try to get it right next time...

Oops!
Mummmmyy!

Don't worry, next time
you must try and tell
someone that you
think you need to go!

TIP: Accidents are very frustrating, but they
are key to learning. A child needs to feel
uncomfortable to help them learn what happens
if they don't find a potty or toilet!

When you need the toilet you will need to know where it is hiding!

Is it behind the curtain?

No! It's here upstairs in the bathroom!

TIP: Make sure your child always knows how to find the toilet, and the different words people use for it.

Before you go, you will need to get undressed.

Just your trousers and pants...

You don't need to take them off completely, just pulling them down is ok!

TIP: Make it easy for your child to get themselves ready for the toilet, no difficult zips or buttons...

Do you know how to sit on the toilet?

I have a special seat and a step stool.

My potty is in the bathroom right next to the loo.

TIP: Make the toilet or potty easy to use, and ready for action. Let them help choose a potty or a seat. Make sure their feet are supported. Knees higher than hips is the perfect position.

Sometimes going to the toilet can take a little while.

I like to read a book.

I like to cuddle my teddy.

TIP: Have a small selection of books or toys for your child to play with while they are on the loo. Take Dolly and her potty along too!

When you have finished you will need to use some toilet paper to clean up.

Just a few sheets will do.

TIP: Teach your child how much paper they need to use, and how to clean up after a wee and a poo. This part can take a long time to master.

Now you are ready to get yourselves dressed again.

Look at my grown up pants!

Mine have princesses on!

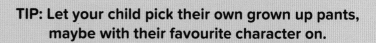

TIP: Let your child pick their own grown up pants, maybe with their favourite character on.

Now it's time to flush it all away.

We are making the toilet nice and clean again... ready for the next person.

TIP: Children can be scared of the noise, especially when out and about. Practice making a flushing noise together and waving off the poo and wee.

Now we must wash and clean our hands.

TIP: Make soap and a towel easy for your child to access.
You might need a step stool too.

Hurray! You did it!

That was nice and easy!

Now you get a reward for doing so well!

TIP: Rewards work best when they are instant, a simple sticker or a small treat.

The End

Now get your child to tell you the story back, using these prompts...

BYE BYE!

YOU DID IT!

Step 1 checklist

- ☐ Are you changing your child's nappy in the bathroom?

- ☐ Are you changing them standing up?

- ☐ Can they help with their own clothing?

- ☐ Do they understand the language - wee and poo, wet and dry?

- ☐ Can they sit on the potty or the toilet?

- ☐ Have you read Poppy and Pablo's big routine together?

- ☐ Have you put the routine in place?

- ☐ Can your child recognise... "I've done a wee."

You are now ready to move to the next step!

Step 2

Signs of readiness

"Sometimes the questions are complicated and the answers are simple." Dr. Seuss

It is important to try and recognise when your child is showing the signs of readiness for potty training. Catching them at the right time can make it easier for you and your child.

There is good reason to suggest that the optimum time is around the age of two and that training later or earlier can significantly extend the time it takes. In addition a child's bladder is also starting to mature at around this age and toilet training itself helps to teach the bladder to develop and hold on.

As children get older, they can become dependent on nappies because they find it more convenient to let a parent clear up the mess than have their play disrupted to go to the toilet. Wearing a nappy becomes a portable potty!

The question we are asked most by parents is "How do I know if my child is ready?" you don't need to tick all the boxes, so look for the general signs, and good engagement in the routine.

It might be as good to ask if you are ready too as potty training does require you to teach your child how to do it. That takes effort, but you will reap the benefits of investing time in the early stages. There is no magic cure that requires no intervention from mum and dad!

Don't be tempted to put it off, delaying when your child is showing some interest can make it much harder later on, as they will have learned to keep on using the nappy, or just lost interest.

Use the assessment chart on the next page to help track when your child is going to the toilet. You can assess if they are doing fewer, larger wees and at regular times. This will help predict when they are likely to need to go. In the early days you can help prompt them at the right time and manage the likelihood of accidents.

What are the signs?

Body

☐ Age - is your child around the age of 2.

☐ Are they doing lots of little wees or fewer big ones (use our chart on page 30 to track).

☐ Physical independence - can they climb the stairs to the bathroom, take down their trousers?

☐ If your child is ill it is a good idea to delay potty training until they are better and able to focus on the task.

Communication

☐ Can they follow simple instructions. (Can you wash your hands?)

☐ Can they make simple requests. (Ask for a drink?)

☐ Do they show signs that they know they are going to do a wee or poo in their nappy? (look out for the potty dance.)

Environment

☐ A stable environment makes it easier for you and your child to focus on the task. Look out for events that would make potty training more difficult...

- Starting school or nursery.
- Moving house.
- Baby expected, or arrived!
- Divorce or separation.

☐ Are you ready too?

Assessment Chart

Keep track of your child's bladder and bowel movements. You are looking for fewer but larger wees, and a pattern to when they go.

This will help you identify your child's readiness to start training by showing they are holding on for longer. It will make it easier to try to predict when you need to encourage your child to sit on the potty when you go for it!

	Example	Day 1	Day 2	Day 3	Day 4	Day 5
Wake up!	Wet nappy					
6am						
7am	Breakfast					
8am	Wet nappy					
9am						
10am						
11am						
Mid-day	Lunch					
1pm	Wet nappy					
2pm						
3pm	Poo					
4pm						
5pm	Supper					
6pm	Wet nappy					
7pm	Bed					
Bed-time!						

Notes

_____

_____

_____

_____

_____

_____

_____

_____

_____

_____

_____

_____

Are you
around the
age of 2 or
above?

Can you
find the
potty or
bathroom?

Can you
wash
your own
hands?

Can
you get
yourself
dressed?

Can you sit
on the potty
or toilet by
yourself?

Sometimes the signs of readiness do not reveal themselves easily, so here are some motivational stories to give you the resolve that you really are ready to move to the next stage and achieve potty training success...

Q. My child made the leap into their own pants but is having lots of accidents everyday. Does this mean that they are not ready to potty train?

No, accidents do not mean that a child is not ready to potty train. Accidents are a key part of learning and all children need to have them in order to learn how to hold on and to recognise their body's signs that they need to go to the toilet. Every child is different and the length of time it takes them to get the hang of it varies depending on lots of factors like the maturity of the bladder. However, most children will be ready around the age of two.

The easiest way to help your child to progress through this stage is to keep them motivated and positive about potty training. Use rewards such as stickers and reward trying as well as success. Try to be patient and aim any frustration at the wee or poo. Keeping a record of when accidents happen can help you pre-empt accidents in the first couple of days, but try not to constantly remind them to sit on the potty, they need to learn that for themselves.

If you have any doubt your child is ready, go back to step one in this book.

Q. My son is not showing any interest in potty training, and wants to keep on wearing nappies. Should I wait until he wants to do it?

Potty training is an important learned skill and won't happen without you intervening and actively taking the steps necessary to train your son. Children are often very happy to wear nappies. It's convenient for them as they don't need to think about taking time out to go to the toilet. Nappies can mask signs of readiness and make it difficult for you both to know when he is going to the toilet.

Instead of waiting for your son to tell you he is ready, we suggest you look for the signs of readiness, as outlined in step 1, and if you think he is ready put in place a good routine and then GO FOR IT.

Q. We have been potty training on and off for a few months. We started again this week and made some good progress but then when we went out I put a nappy back on. Is this the wrong thing to do?

The fact your little one had shown success is a great sign. Yes, popping a nappy back on can be confusing as they can't feel when they have had an accident and it gives your little one an option to get out of potty training if he wants!

We suggest you start by putting in place a good routine, and if he is showing signs of readiness then it's time to say 'bye bye' to the nappy for good. Once you remove the nappy in the daytime, it should not go back on. Although you don't want to delay potty training if he is ready, check that you start at a time when you have the time to be able to commit to potty training and accidents. For example, starting the week after a new baby is born or during his first week in a new nursery would add unnecessary stress to everyone.

Q. My son hates the potty and refuses to sit on it, how can we start training when I can't get him near it?

You could try to make the potty more appealing to him by covering it in stickers or let him try sitting on a child's seat on the toilet. Make sure he is comfortable and use incentives and lots of praise for practicing sitting there. Start with short periods then use toys or books to distract him and encourage him to stay there for longer.

Introduce toilet time into his normal daily routine and teach him that this is an important task that is not optional.

If you are still not having any luck, you may need to enlist the help of another adult such as a family friend or Health Visitor to explain to him that he needs to practice sitting on the potty and then reward him when he does.

Q. My daughter is doing really well at training but always asks for a nappy to poo in. If I don't give her one, she keeps on holding it in which worries me.

It is important that your child doesn't get used to holding on to their poo as this can lead to complications. Let her have a nappy to poo in. Keep it in the bathroom and tell her she needs to remain in the bathroom while she does it. Then remove the nappy and flush the poo away while she is still there. The next stage is to get her to poo in the nappy while sitting on the toilet and then you can move towards removing the nappy altogether.

Hey. if we all think we're ready, let's go for it!

Step 3

GOING FOR IT!

"Believe you can and you're halfway there."

Theodore Roosevelt

When you decide to GO FOR IT! Take the nappy off and do not be tempted to put it back on. It can confuse your child when they are just starting out, and it can also make them believe that they have a choice.

At this stage you are only taking the nappy off in the day. Night time potty training comes later.

If the leap is too great, use Dry Like Me pads to help to capture the mess and remove the temptation to put the nappy back on. Remember you can't potty train in a nappy, therefore you must make the leap into their own pants.

Toilet training is all about learning to hold on, and to listen to your body's signals, it's not an easy skill to master, and can be stressful for children too.

Accidents are a key part of learning, your child may not have felt the difference between wet and dry in their nappy. The only way they can learn is through trial and error, which will mean lots of accidents in the early days.

Young children can only feel that they need the toilet when their bladder is about ¾ full, and therefore accidents are large and there is less time to react. They will get better at predicting and holding on as their bladder and their brains connect and mature.

Lots of praise and rewards in the early stages are essential, and will help teach your child to learn the right toilet training behaviours. We recommend instant rewards that are small and inexpensive for maximum impact. (Use the stickers in this book).

Try not to get frustrated, if they don't appear to be succeeding, focus praise on effort in trying and the parts of potty training that are going well, such as washing hands. Aim your frustration at the naughty wee or poo, and get your child to join in. It will help re assert what is expected next time, and that they are not to blame.

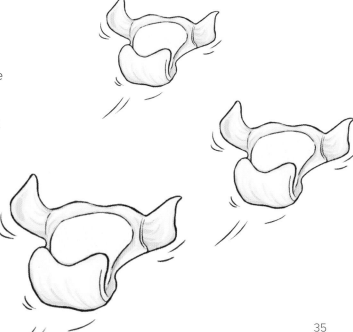

BYE BYE NAPPY!

Tips for success

Make a big fuss of ditching the nappies with your child, and picking their own grown up pants.
Make it a special "bye bye nappy day!".

Communicate clearly what is expected of them, and keep re affirming this.

Be prepared for lots of accidents especially in the early stages, and remember this is actually progress although it won't feel like it! Make sure you have LOTS of grown up pants, wipes, and towels.

Choose clothes that are easy to manage with no tricky fastenings, and that are easy to wash and dry too.

Use instant rewards – stickers are excellent as they can be put straight on the child - use the ones in this book!

If you are putting a reward chart up, pop it in the bathroom so that the reward is nearby.

Consistency – use the same language to describe wees and poos, and make everyone aware that you are potty training!

KEEP CALM! Use Poppy and Pablo's big routine as a corner stone to your potty training efforts, and to reinforce what is expected.

Introduce "Toilet time!" make it a normal part of your child's daily routine.

Keep an eye on your child's mannerisms you may notice the signs they are ready to go before they do. Watch out for the potty dance!

Diet and good hydration are really important to enable good body functions. Use our "What goes in must come out" section to explain to your child all about how to be healthy.

Try not to constantly tell them to go to the toilet. Part of potty training is learning the feeling of when to go for yourself and being made to go before you reach this stage can prolong training. The odd reminder at key times when accidents have a tendency to occur is preferable.

In hot weather it can be tempting to let children run around without any pants on, but it can mean a step back and accidents when they need to start wearing pants and undressing themselves before getting on the potty.

The goal at the end of this stage is that your child is successfully getting most wees and poos in the toilet or potty, and that they can clearly identify that...

I am doing a wee.

How your body works

READ TOGETHER

I make sure I eat lots of different coloured healthy foods, and drink lots of water!'

Food & Water goes in

∨

Down to your tummy

∨

Your body uses the best bits to make you big & strong

∨

The rest travels down to your bottom and comes out as poo or wee

Bye Bye wee and poo and thank you for the good stuff!

> What goes in must come out.

Poppy and Pablo's potty training picnic

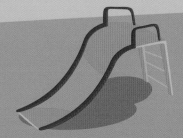

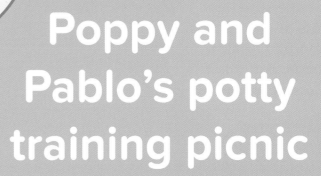

Kids love picnics, and they encourage them to eat healthy, raw fresh foods.

This keeps bladder and bowel healthy and so keeps potty training on track.

Picnic Pic 'n' mix

Carrot, pepper & cucumber sticks
Chopped up cheese
Grapes and apple
Strawberries and raspberries
Kiwis to eat with a teaspoon
Pitta pockets
Homemade chocolate crispy cakes
using wholewheat puffed rice

What else can you think of
to take to your picnic?

Tips

Keep hydrated in the summer and when colds and flu are around as they can dehydrate too.

Freeze fruit juices and smoothies into lollies to get lots of vitamins in!

Use the summer to encourage lots of healthy salad vegetables and crudités.

Have a wide and varied diet.

Eat lots of different coloured foods, lots of variety and everything in moderation.

Don't over do the fibre as this can irritate some children's tummies.

Here are some words that Poppy and Pablo use.

Toilet

Potty

Tinkle

Poop

Loo

Piddle

Wee wee

Number two

What words do you use? Add your own here...

Step 3 checklist

☐ Did you take the nappy off?

☐ Did you do your first wee on the potty?

☐ Did you do your first poo on the potty?

☐ Are you learning to hold on?

☐ Can you ask when you need to go?

☐ Have you gone a whole day without an accident?

☐ Can you tell "I am going to the toilet I need it now!"

You are now ready to move to the next step!

Step 4

Keeping it going!

"Life is like riding a bicycle. To keep your balance, you must keep moving."

Albert Einstein

This stage is all about potty training in the real world, when the spotlight has come off the first couple of weeks of intensive training, and the distractions of every day life are all around.

This is the time when you are most likely to think things are not working, and be tempted to put a nappy back on.

At this stage your child is:

• Learning to hold on for longer, and telling you when they need to go in advance.
• Being motivated to go without the need for constant rewards and without being reminded.
• Learning to listen to their bodies when distracted by play.
• Having the confidence to ask to go to the toilet when they are away from their own home, or at school or nursery.

Look out for signs that your child is tired, as this is a common time for accidents, and give them gentle reminders and extra encouragement. Remember they will forget to listen to their body when they are tired, they are unlikely to be doing it on purpose.

Tips

First trips out – be prepared, take changes of clothes, a potty in a carrier bag, and make first trips short and achievable.

Make people that you are visiting aware of your expectations, especially if your child is going without you. Where possible make sure that they follow your system.

Expect accidents when on play dates, or at school. They are learning an additional skill – to listen to their bodies while they are busy and distracted.

If there is a common time or situation that they have accidents, look out for tiredness, and heap extra praise and attention on keeping dry during this period.

Try to keep positive. Your child can get frustrated and frightened of failure at this stage, especially after doing so well earlier on.

Make sure you know where the toilets are when you are out and about. Talk to them about the noise of hand dryers, and the need to queue!

Be consistent, the good foundations are in place and you are nearly there!

I need a wee.

At the end of this stage you are looking for your child to be able to recognise they need the toilet, and if it is urgent or not. They will be saying...

"I need a wee" and to be able to identify if they can hold on or not.

What to expect when you are out and about

Some toilets flush differently to home. You wave your hand in front of this one...

Hand dryers can be very noisy. They may look like this.

There are boys toilets and girls toilets.
You will go to either with *your mummy and daddy*
or to a special toilet with a change mat.
(but that's for babies in nappies!).

There are lots of different signs that show you that there is a toilet.

You will probably need to queue, sometimes for a long time, so make sure you say as soon as possible that you need to go!

Toilets have locks on, this helps people know you are in there.

Toilets are in cubicles, but everyone shares the sinks!

Step 4 checklist

☐ Have I been on a first trip out with my grown up pants on?

☐ Have I been to nursery with my grown up pants on?

☐ Have I asked to go to the toilet while out and about?

☐ Have I been out shopping and held on?

☐ Have I put my hand up at nursery and asked a teacher to go to the toilet?

☐ Have I been on a play date with my grown up pants on?

Well done. You have officially cracked it!

Certificate of achievement

This is to congratulate

On officially being a star potty trainer!

WELL DONE!

You're a star!

Poppy
xx

Pablo

Step 5

Night time potty training

"A day without sunshine is like, you know, night."

Steve Martin

Once you have mastered day time potty training, you are ready to tackle night time potty training.

Look out for plenty of dry nappies in the morning as a sign that they are learning to hold on through the night.

Buy the right kit, accidents at night are exhausting for everyone, so make sure you are prepared. Protect the bed with a waterproof bed mat. Make sure there are fresh pyjamas nearby.

Keep your child in clothing that will be easy to pull down or up to do a wee.

Make sure the potty is by the bed or easily accessible and well lit. Some children are frightened to get up and go to the toilet at night.

Night time potty training is about listening to your body when you are very tired and sleepy, learning to hold on for even longer stretches (maybe up to 12 hours).

Bedwetting is a common problem, and may not resolve until your child is around seven. This is because the bladder is still maturing. If you suspect this is the case talk to your health professional. You can find excellent help and advice at **howtopottytrain.co.uk**

Guide to potty training at night.

Limit drinks in the early evening, about an hour before bedtime. Limit squashes and acidic drinks that can irritate the bladder.

Encourage visiting the toilet as part of the normal bedtime routine and before lights go out.

Communicate what you are trying to do, and that they need to try and listen to their bodies at night as well as in the day.

Make sure the potty is easily accessible, put a towel or bedmat underneath to catch any spillages.

For the first couple of weeks lift them at night so they can do a "dream wee" while their bladder learns to hold on for two long stretches at night. Gently lift your child onto the potty or toilet around 10-11pm. They should easily wee without fully waking up.

If your child does wake for whatever reason, ask if they need to go to the toilet, to make sure their bladder is completely empty. Ask even if they have had an accident.

Keep a night light on, so that your child can find the toilet or potty easily, and isn't scared.

Read Lilly and Luca's bedtime story to help set the scene...

Lilly and Luca's Bedtime story

Lilly and Luca are getting
ready for bed.

Only a small drink
tonight Lilly – we are
going to be big girls
and boys!

Before we go to bed we need to...

Brush our teeth.

Wash our face.

AND....Go to the toilet!

TIP: It is important to reward effort and trying at night time, as despite trying, some children will continue to have accidents and it is not their fault, their bladder is just not ready.

Thanks and further support

We have worked with many health professionals and helped many parents with advice since 2008 and we have accumulated a lot of good advice and concepts. Here are some key people whose ideas we would like to acknowledge.

June Rogers MBE for her support in when toilet training gets tricky. In particular the idea of a "poo nappy" the concept that after normal potty training age, children no longer need a nappy but use it as a convenience or 'portable toilet'.

Dr Eve Fleming - her early work with us helped establish firmly the concept of a good routine and sequencing as the foundation to all good potty training.

Find out more...

June Rogers MBE - Children's continence advisor and team director at PromoCon - www.promocon.co.uk

ERIC (Education and Resources for Improving Childhood Continence) - www.eric.org.uk
UK charity which supports children and their families with potty training, bedwetting, daytime wetting, soiling and constipation.

The National Autistic Society - www.autism.org.uk

Our team at Dry Like Me - www.drylikeme.com

Also find out more at www.howtopottytrain.co.uk

Thanks to...

Marie and Mark at Spring Corporation.

Sharon Harmer at Moo Art.

Alan and Alistair at Brewin Books.

Paul and Andrew. James, Matt and Chris.

Special thanks to our families and friends who have lived potty training well beyond the usual years.

David, Stuart, Pam and Robin, and Janet and Tony.

Finally to the ultimate inspiration...

Harry, Heather, Grace and Matilda.

Well done Lilly and Luca!

The End